Christopher has worked as a classroom teacher for over 30 years. His experience ranges from inner-city mainstream schools to special education needs and disability schools for pupils with challenging behaviour. He has taught from year 1 to year 11. Throughout his career, he stayed committed to classroom teaching, loving the creative challenge of directly teaching pupils.

Over the years, he developed the ideas contained in this book. They worked for him and so he shared them with his colleagues. His behaviour-management programme was successful in every area of teaching. Now he shares his behaviour-management techniques with you.

To Jane

Chris

This book is dedicated to all the pupils I have taught.

Christopher Ayton

BEHAVIOUR

AUSTIN MACAULEY PUBLISHERS™

LONDON • CAMBRIDGE • NEW YORK • SHARJAH

A CIP catalogue record for this title is available from the British Library.

ISBN 9781528906395 (Paperback)
ISBN 9781528906401 (Hardback)
ISBN 9781528906418 (Kindle e-book)
ISBN 9781528958271 (ePub e-book)

www.austinmacauley.com

First Published (2019)
Austin Macauley Publishers Ltd
25 Canada Square
Canary Wharf
London
E14 5LQ

Thank you all at Austin Macauley Publishers for giving me this opportunity to publish my book and for your support and encouragement. I'm indebted to my friends who encouraged me to write and made my writing accessible to the rest of humanity. To all the pupils I have taught, thank you, without you this book wouldn't exist. Nicky and Angie, your support and encouragement means more to me than anything else, I love you dearly.

Excellent Classroom Behaviour
(in six weeks).
Guaranteed
(or your money back).

This is not a book about the theory of child behaviour or an analysis of why kids mess about in your lessons. No, this is a book that will get the kids in your class behaving the way you want them to behave, and if you follow the programme I lay down in this book, you will have the pupils in your class eating out of your hand in six weeks...

I'm not a professor in child educational psychology or some educationalist who spent two weeks in the reception class because they got lost on their way to Sainsbury's and ended up in the nursery, managed to find their way to the reception class but lost the ability to walk, collapsed in the girls' toilets to be found by a four-year-old, who took them to the administration office and then out of the main doors and freedom.

No, I'm a teacher, a real live teacher, teaching right now in a primary class in an inner city school. I have taught for 30 years. All my teaching experience has been as a classroom teacher. I have taught all the year groups from nursery to Year 6. I have also worked as a supply teacher and in a Pupil Referral Unit (PRU), a school for children with behavioural challenges.

What I am about to show you is not based on some theory or some dogmatic ideology. Like the teacher training you have been on, or the useless training used to fill the time allocated as "Training Days". Sitting thinking, 'What the hell am I doing here when I could be doing something useful in the classroom, get that display finished or marking those books that I haven't marked for over a term, or input that assessment data that should have been done two weeks ago.' This book is based on real-life tried and tested ideas that do work.

I have taken all the most useful stuff from all the different training, from the books I've read and my own personal experience and discussion with my colleagues, and what I have here is a proven way that I use to this day, and it has been tried and tested over and over again in many different situations with different year groups. Follow my advice and your class will be the best behaved class in the school; not only will their behaviour improve but also their academic results. But this book is not about improving academic success, that comes automatically from the improved behaviour of your pupils. No, this book is about improving the behaviour of the children in your class. You won't like much of what I tell you to do. I don't like it myself, but I have found it works, so I do it. You have a choice – follow your trendy, liberal ideas and have kids that are going to make your life hell every single day. They will also make life hell for the vulnerable children in your class and you will either last about three to five years in teaching, then get a job in Tesco filling shelves with baked beans or if you are lucky, you'll get promoted out of the classroom and you can spend the rest of your teaching career telling other teachers how to manage behaviour, although you were useless at doing behaviour management when you were in the classroom, hence why you went for that promotion in the first place.

Don't feel a failure if you can't handle the kids in your class, it isn't your fault. It is your management's fault. They, the management of your school, have not got a clue how to manage behaviour. If they did, they would be able to advise you, and the advice they give you would work. The reason you are reading this book is because the advice they gave you was shite. Your kids are still messing about and ruining your lessons, disrupting your classroom, bullying each other and ignoring you. Follow my advice in this book and all that will stop. I guarantee it.

At this point I want to clarify the breadth of this book in relation to the impact it will have. This book is aimed at the improvement of behaviour for 95% for your children. The 5% of children that are outside the mainstream will need a moderated version of the advice I will give you and for some children it won't work. The one or two kids in your class who really should have 'one-to-one' support but don't get it because it takes 20 years to get a statement or the Special Educational Needs and Disabilities (SEND) teacher is a buffoon, spending all their time in endless child conferences, drinking tea and chatting about how to make the best Victoria sponge cake, while the kid they are all having their ever-so-important meeting about is throwing chairs around in your writing session. But to be honest, even these children can improve their behaviour with a moderated version of what is contained in this book. I will give you some guidance on how to moderate the advice to individualise this behaviour programme for those children who seem to be uncontrollable.

Let me quickly say here that throughout this book, I use the term "playtime" or "break time". This means any time that your students are not in a lesson. I also use the term "sad face" to denote a sanction (this will become clearer later); obviously you do not have to use a "sad face" symbol to denote displeasure, you could use a "skull and cross bones" symbol or an emoji. It's up to you, it's your class room or lesson.

You need two things to have excellent behaviour in your classroom.

One: an effective reward system. A reward system based on rewards that the children want, not what you think they should have. So a reward system that rewards children by giving them an apple will fail.

Two: clear and definable expectations. Your expectations need to be a development over time, see your behaviour management as a process, give yourself at least eight weeks before you assess the behaviour of your children in your class. Start by identifying one behaviour that you want to improve, for example, "listening to the teacher". Focus on that behaviour, then move on to something like "listening to your peers". Then maybe "focusing on your work". Firstly, stay focused for five minutes, then ten, then fifteen minutes. Always see your behaviour management as a process, don't think you are going to walk into a class and all the kids are going to respect you and do what you tell them to do first time. That is not going to happen.

Where to Start

First, the beginning of every session must always have the classroom set out ready for work. Therefore, the pupils' desk should have work ready. Anything will do, it doesn't have to do with the actual lesson you are about to teach, just a piece of work that they can get on with as soon as they enter the classroom. A worksheet is good or some work they were doing in a previous session, but it must be something they can get on with without your intervention. A colouring sheet or simple Maths worksheet. Obviously you can tailor it for your children in your class.

Have the work placed in each child's place with a pen or pencil next to it ready to use. Sharpen the pencils or have pens that work. You can give a child the job of setting up the classroom this way at each break time. As you know, there are always children wanting to do "jobs". Now you have jobs to give them. A word of warning on giving "jobs" to children: do not leave the children alone in the class, even the most well behaved children will do stupid stuff while alone with their mates. Also, the children doing the classroom "jobs" should do it in silence. You want to maintain at all times a calm and quiet environment in your classroom. If the children who are putting out the books and pencils for you are rowdy, you have created a rowdy situation before your class has even entered the classroom.

Your management and other so-called advisors who come to you and your school boasting about their years of teaching, and all the books they have written and the government ministers they advise, will tell you all sorts of bollocks. One of their obsessions: "displays". You'll go to your Head and let them know that you are struggling with this or that child. They will look at you and say, 'Is the Maths display finished?' What the hell! I am telling you now, whatever the so-called educational experts say, displays do not improve classroom behaviour and on a more controversial note, I don't believe they improve academic success either. We all know of that teacher and teaching assistant (TA) that are super arty and do the most magnificent "displays". Their displays are works of art that should be on display in the Tate or some other art gallery. Do their kids behave well? Are the kids in their class more successful than in other classes? No, they aren't; that's not to say that your classroom should not be a nice, inviting environment. But all this nonsense about displays is crap. The reason heads and the like put pressure on you and the TA to have displays that rival Michelangelo, is that displays are tangible and visible. They can see if you have done it or not, and most managers haven't a clue about how to manage behaviour. Hence, they deflect their lack of knowledge and skill on to other irrelevant nonsense.

Another stick they like to beat us with is our lessons. They tell us, the reason your kids are behaving in an inappropriate way is because your lessons are boring. Look, it doesn't matter if a lesson is boring or exciting, if you are a kid, it is much more fun to mess about, and annoy other children and yourself, than engage with the lesson. So don't accept that the reason for unacceptable behaviour is your fault or that your lessons are boring. Children are able to behave in an appropriate way whatever the lesson is like, boring or not. So what if a lesson is boring? Not everything can be exciting in life; at the end of the day, teachers are here to teach, not to entertain the children in our class. School is not a pantomime where teachers are the entertainment. So, when your Head comes at you with that one, tell them to piss off. I know you won't do that but you should, or ask them to provide the evidence that a so-called "boring" lesson impacts on academic achievement. Also, what is "boring"? I actually know people who think football is boring!

The Classroom

The children entering your classroom is a critical point in the day; almost everything will stem from that moment in time. So spend time getting that part of the day right and do it every time the children enter your classroom. At the beginning of the day, after break, after dinner and after assembly or P.E. or any time the pupils re-enter the room.

Note that I said "your classroom". It is your classroom, not the head teacher's or any other line manager you have. You have total control over what happens in "your" classroom. Heads and their management team have a strategic responsibility for the school. They do not have any power to force you to teach in a particular way or force you to mark your books in any particular way. They try to bully us into accepting their moronic nonsense. That is for their benefit, not ours. It is to show Ofsted or any other body that they are fantastic head teachers or managers. We do the work and they get the credit. One major problem with their interfering, controlling approach is that it has the effect of undermining the classroom teacher. Both in the eyes of the pupils and the teacher themselves, who feel that they do not have ownership of their own situation. That is a dangerous situation for management to create because it leads to teachers not having the emotional strength in their own classroom. To have good behaviour management, the teacher has to be clearly, and without reservation, the one and only leader in that classroom. You are the classroom, everything that happens in that room is down to you, you are the King, the Queen, the God of that room. Nothing moves or is said or happens without you knowing about it. I know that's bollocks, but you have to project that persona to the children.

Children need to feel safe and protected. If you don't offer that, then the class bully offers it. If the child complies with the bully, then the bully won't bully them. They will go bully someone else. Remember this, you can't have socialism in one country and so you can't have socialism in one classroom. We live in a bullying, racist, sexist, oppressive society, and children are the most oppressed. This is their world, it is not our world. If you want to live in a world of freedom, justice and equality, then change the world, you can't do it one classroom at a time. So forget your well-intentioned quest for equality. Here, in the classroom, you are the boss, like it or not. If you can't play that role, don't teach.

In the classroom, you set the boundaries, the tone, the expectations. You can do it, you don't have to believe in it or even like it, but you do have to do it, if you want your children to behave in an appropriate way. Failure to own your classroom will lead to a failure of behaviour management. You kids will prat about all day, every day.

Rules

My favourite rule is: "For every negative thing I say, I will say three positive things". I live by this rule. It is fundamental to all I will tell you: remember it, write it somewhere, tattoo it on your arm, have it as a screen saver, anything, but remember it and do it. I will get back to that, but firstly, making negative comments to children. It is a skill, you will come across some fools who will tell you that teachers should not be negative, that is a load of shite. Negativity is much stronger that positivity. Think about it. If you are about to cross the road and in the corner of your eye you see a bus, you stop. Fear of being squashed by the 192 bus stopped you and probably saved your life. The 192 bus stops for no man or woman for that matter, but if by some quirk of nature, seeing the 192 bus out of the corner of your eye fills you with joy and wondrous love for buses travelling at speed, you sense little or no danger, you continue to cross. Why wouldn't you? You are getting feelings of happiness and contentment. Bang! You are dead. So let me tell you now, don't think you are going to go through your teaching career never saying anything negative. You will, but there are ways to be negative. There is the right way and the wrong way. "You are stupid for hitting that girl" – wrong. "Hitting that girl is stupid" – better. Though try to avoid the word stupid, people get really upset about it. I love the word stupid, it sounds great and I like the look of it, but people get really stupid about the word stupid.

Back to my example, the first way of being negative is making a negative comment about that child. You are saying that they are stupid. They probably are but you don't want them to think that about themselves. However, you do want them to think that the behaviour they engaged in was stupid and unacceptable. The second way I said the negative comment says that the behaviour was stupid, not the child.

Your task as a teacher is to create a positive learning environment. You can do that, you have to do that, not by displays and marking policies or neat books, but by your relationship with the children. Avoid the word "wrong". What you believe to be "wrong", a child will not; "wrong" and "right" are subjective. Some people thought it was wrong to drop an atomic bomb on an unsuspecting city, other people thought it was right to drop an atomic bomb on an unsuspecting city. Behaviour is either unacceptable or inappropriate or acceptable and appropriate, use those words. Even to younger children, they may not understand the meaning but they will pick up on the positive and negative connotations of the words.

"Hitting that girl is inappropriate". OK, you have made a negative comment, you have not made a negative comment about the child, it was about their behaviour, and you have not made a moralistic judgement about their behaviour, therefore you haven't judged them, but you have made a negative comment. So, now you have to make three positive comments straight away. You do not make a positive comment about the child who has just displayed inappropriate behaviour. That would send a mixed message to the child. It must be to other children and within earshot of the offending child. If you can be positive to a child whom you know that the child you have just been negative to admires, or is best friends with or is in a friendship group with, even better. The positive comment can be for anything. "Well done, James, you are breathing"; "I like the way you hold your pencil, Sarah"; "That is excellent sitting, Adam".

Now at this point, you want to reinforce your positive comment with a reward. I will talk about reward systems later, also have some type of team reward system. So that when you give the positive comment, give a team point or whatever reward system you use. Your positive comments mean points or rewards of some kind. Use physical reinforcement of your positiveness. You have to overcome the power of negativeness, positiveness needs to be stronger, but actually in nature it is not. Humans survived because of our ability to recognise negative situations quickly and respond to them, not positive ones. You can survive without an orgasm but you can't survive if a lion eats you. But the main part to remember is: "For every negative comment, you say three positive comments." I do this shit every day; without fail, it works.

Classroom Setup

How to set out your classroom for effective teaching, learning and behaviour management? "Carpet time" – it is bollocks. So don't do it. Maybe for young children to listen to a story or for some type of discussion-type activity. But from Year 3 upwards, do not do it. You have the kids all sitting nicely on their chairs, working away, and then all of a sudden, it's "carpet time", to discuss the next problem or to introduce a topic or whatever it is you feel the need to have the kids sat on their arses for half an hour while you prattle on with yourself. You can very effectively talk to and discuss with the children in your class while they are sat on their seats. There is no need to add into your day extra excuses for your kids to hit, kick, punch, slap, step on, sit on or puke on someone. NO, if the children are sat and ready to learn, then leave them where they are. Try to avoid too much movement for the kids. Having said that, there are ways to move children that reduce the amount of disruption and unwanted disruptive behaviour.

Lining Up

Lining children up to leave the classroom or moving from assembly to the classroom or from the classroom to the hall or from the classroom to the playground for playtime or to the hall for dinner time, P.E., home time or whatever. Decide where they will line up, from the door of the classroom, and the line runs along the wall or the window or in front of the white board. You`decide this and you tell the children. The children do not decide this; it is your classroom so you tell the children where they line up. Seems a bit petty but it reinforces the idea that you are in control in the classroom. *

Have rules on how they line up. Number one rule: no talking in the line. The children should only be in the line for a few minutes, so the no-talking rule shouldn't be a big deal. Explain this: "You will be in the line for two minutes while we walk outside to the playground, then you can talk all you want". It's natural for people to talk and to talk once we have finished something, to discuss it or work through it. Therefore, children will want to do that too. So why not allow talking while moving from place to place? Because there are key trigger points during your day and moving from place to place is a trigger point. It is a trigger point for disruptive behaviour. Think about it, the students are moving from a structured activity to what could be an unstructured activity. You want the lining up of your pupils to be structured so that your well-maintained, orderly class stays that way until they get to the place they need to be. Moving a group of pupils can be very problematic; don't allow it to become problematic, keep control of the situation.

It is a good idea to identify your trigger points. For example, cloakrooms, toilets, any "out of sight" spots either in your classroom or outside, the corridor and of course, the playground. You'll have your own trigger points for your children in your school. If you think about it now, I bet you can think of at least three trigger points, right off the top of your head. Once you have identified your trigger areas, then follow some of the tips I'm giving you to eradicate any behaviour issues.

Back to lining up. While lining up there is no talking; children should have their arms folded. Why? Because if the children fold their arms, they can't poke, hit, slap, pull down, pinch or push or steal. We now have two rules for lining up, no talking and fold your arms.

How to line the children up? How you line the pupils up sets the tone for how your line of children will behave. Say to a whole class "line up" and you'll have a riot. The children will push and shove, some will use the unstructured time to steal someone's pen or pencil or hat. Then you'll have to spend the next hour sorting all that out. Obviously, once you have all your expectations in place, then you need to have an effective reward system. I'll talk about that later. Now, lining the children up. You have told them what they must do in the line, "No talking and folded arms". You select a table where the children are sitting, select a table that has children you know will probably do as you have asked. Let them line up first, just the one table of children, while the rest of the class is sat in silence watching. This is all happening in silence, so you will need to have your class completely silent while you line the children up. The first group of children line up. You are watching them, the rest of the class sit and watch too. If these children line up without talking and have their arms folded, then you choose the next group of children to line up. However, if any of the children talk, you sit the offending child down, do not warn them. You have already told them your expectation. It is not unreasonable to tell the offending child to leave the line and sit down. You have the right as a teacher to tell them to behave in a certain way for a limited time to aid the effective learning of the children and this will do that, because you won't need to waste your time sorting out rubbish. Lining up the children the way you want them to line up gets them to break time or wherever they need to be in a few minutes. Once they have mastered the art of lining up, they get more playtime or break time, you get a longer break and the children are happy and ready to learn when they get back. If at any time, while you are lining up the children, you find that a number of the children are talking or not folding their arms and you are not able to identify the culprits, then sit the whole line back down in their seats, explain that you had to sit everyone down, even the people who were getting it "right" and you don't like doing that, but you had no choice because you couldn't see the people who were talking. Then start the lining up process again; the kids soon get sick of lining up and sitting down. They want to get out to play or break or in the hall or wherever, so they soon start to line up the way you want.

Now, walking around the school as a class.

Walking Around the School

To walk your class to and fro, you need clear and simple rules. These are your walking around the school rules. The children walk in a line, that may seem obvious to you and me but to a child a line can be anything from a disorganised gaggle to a mark on a piece of paper. Tell the children that a line means that they have to walk one behind the other. Think that is easy? Kids find it almost impossible to do it. I don't blame them really, walking around looking at the back of someone's neck is not pleasant, but it has to be done. Unless of course you don't mind a small riot each time you leave your classroom and walk to assembly.

One big mistake a lot of teachers make is where they position themselves while walking the kids around the school. Most teachers go striding off in the front of the line of kids in the false hope that the kids will meekly walk along behind them in some sense of order. "You have got your back to the kids, they will mess about". If you are lucky enough to have a TA, then you the teacher stay about halfway down the line of children. That way you can see the line of kids in front of you, and your TA walks near the rear of the line. There, you have the whole class covered.

You do need to move along the line while walking kids around the school or to and from a place. Don't think that because you are out of the classroom you are on a break. NO, it is harder work outside the classroom than in it. Have your "reward stickers" on you at all times. I will talk about how to give your "reward stickers" meaning, in other words, how to make your pupils want your reward stickers. I will do that later, but for now, use your stickers to reward the children who are following your expectations. They should be walking in a line, silent and with arms folded. As your line of children leave your classroom, once you have got them silent and lined up, give a sticker to every child as they walk past you; as the middle of the line nears, give stickers to a few more children then allow your TA to give out stickers to those at the back of the line. You walk to the front of the line, face along the line giving out stickers again; as the middle of the line nears again, walk to near the front and walk backwards facing the children as they walk past you giving out stickers to all the children following your expectations.

Your line of children should have "stopping points". Stopping points are places along your route to the hall, playground or park or yard, that have been predetermined by you and are known to the children. The stopping points allow you to maintain the line so that it doesn't become too stretched out and the children start to sidle up to each other, begin chatting and shouting then fighting. At each stopping point, allow the line to stop. The instruction to the children is "Next stopping point". The line will walk from stopping point to stopping point.

The stopping point idea also helps your control of the pupils' behaviour. It reinforces the idea that you tell the children what to do and they do it. They want to get out to play or break, so they conform by following your instructions while walking around the school – it becomes increasingly what they do. They listen to you and do as you tell them.

I have used the "next stopping point" idea of walking around school with children who display challenging behaviour. I've got them to walk around the school with me telling them to go to the next stopping point. I have given them an instruction and they have followed it. They don't realise that this is what they are doing, so it becomes something they just do. It is an unconscious compliance to your instruction. It doesn't work instantly or just on its own, you will need to follow my whole behaviour programme for it to work effectively, but it is a weapon in your behaviour armoury.

I use the "next stopping point" idea when I am walking my class to many places. When I walk them to the swimming baths or to the local museum or local park, I use street lampposts as markers for the next stopping point. Always place a reliable student at the front of your line of students. Tell the pupil at the front of the line, "When you get to that next lamppost, stop". Make sure they can see the lamppost and that you are confident that they will stop at the said lamppost. In effect, when you are walking your students from place to place outside of the school grounds, you are stopping at each lamppost to allow the line of pupils to gather together. Lines of pupils always straggle out over an increasing distance. The distance from the front of the line to the back of the line grows as the class of students walks along the street. The "stopping point" concept allows you to gather your pupils together and maintain control.

How to Get Children to Listen

Getting your kids to shut up is hard. You can shout very loudly, but you can only do that a few times and then your voice becomes sore and eventually you lose your voice altogether. Also, to shout to get quietness loses the impact somewhat. If you really have to shout, due to something very important like telling a kid not to call Ahemd "a knobhead", then do it with feeling. The general rule is, you want to use your voice as little as possible.

Teachers that prattle on are boring and ineffectual. I'm not saying don't shout or talk. Sometimes it is necessary to shout, but you will be told by your management that you should never shout. That is bollocks. Shouting is a bit like using a car, not desirable but sometimes necessary.

Shouting isn't an effective method to get your kids to be quiet. The standard sticking-your-hand-in-the-air is my preferred method. If you have no idea what I am talking about, I will explain it to you. Here goes: you stand at the front of the class, you stand still, you put your hand in the air. This is the zero noise sign. You have already explained to the children that whenever they see you with your hand in the air, they have to copy you. Next, also tell them that when your hand is in the air, it means zero noise. In other words, when your hand is in the air, they stop talking. Sounds simple and also sounds like it wouldn't work in your class. It works, not straight away, but it works. When you want to give the class an instruction, the pupils are busy talking about their work, my arse they are, but we can pretend. You stand at the front of the class and confidently put your hand in the air. You do not talk, you do not say "I have my hand in the air". You say nothing, you wait and wait. One kid notices, who looks at you, then they put their hand in the air, another kid, then another, then eventually they all have their hand in the air, the talking slowly subsiding.

Listen, it's not going to happen like this the first time you do it, especially if the kids have never come across this method of getting them to shut up. But it will work if you insist. You may well have to sanction children that do not follow the rule of hand in the air – zero noise. However, in time it will work. You can also reward pupils that do follow your example by giving them "team points" as you stand waiting for silence (more on this later). Do not do what most teachers do, which is to put their hand in the air and start shouting, "Put your hand up, Peter"; "Jenny, put your hand up and shut up"; "Muaz, shut up and put your hand up". Defeats the purpose, if you choose to use the hand up for zero noise method; do it the way I have explained it to you.

One last thing, you are standing at the front of the class with your hand in the air, the children are carrying on talking. Turn to the whiteboard with your marker in hand. Look at a child that is talking; it doesn't matter if they look back, they know you are looking at them. Then very slowly turn to the whiteboard and write their name on the board under the "sad face" (we call this "name on the board"; more about this later). You still have your hand in the air. The other children will notice what you have done and start to put their hands up. Wait a few seconds if they are not responding quickly enough. Then look at another child that is talking, turn slowly and write their name on the whiteboard under the "sad face". I will talk more about name on the board as a sanction later.

There will be times when you want a silent class, usually when you are hung over or still pissed. Don't think teachers don't turn up in school still pissed from the night before, apparently. One school I worked in, the assistant head, allegedly, was always on the razz and regularly turned up in school still inebriated. Her TA would tell her to go and get her head down in the head's office to sleep it off. This she did while the TA took the class, allegedly. I am not suggesting you go to school pissed, stoned or out of your head on coke, although it happens, apparently. Back to a silent class, there are times when it is useful for the class to work in silence. If you really want the pupils to work independently, I would suggest the best way to guarantee this is to have the children work in silence. If they are silent, the kids can't be telling each other the answers or helping each other. That is not to say that helping each other and working together to solve problems isn't a good way to teach. But there are times when you need the children to work independently so that you know exactly what each child is capable of. You have got to remember that the one thing that the English education system is brilliant at producing is expert and proficient copiers. Every child in our schools is just excellent at copying. A child can be sitting at the other end of the class and still be able to copy the answer to a question. If only the international index of quality education included copying, then the English education system would be top draw.

Times when I used silent working were when pupils are redrafting and were at the point where they are writing up their final copy after correcting and editing their work. Handwriting is nice in silence and pupils like a time of quiet too. Independent assessment, I would usually have in silence. Do not be afraid to use a silent classroom; classrooms do not always have to be noisy for them to be productive and enjoyable for the pupils and teacher.

If the kids are all working away independently in silence, what are you going to be doing? Well, if you have your TA with you at the time, which probably you won't because she or he will probably be taken off you to cover for an absent teacher in another class or to cover for Planning Preparation and Assessment (PPA) or to run an errand for the head, then on the rare occasions when both you and your TA are in the classroom together and the children are all working independently, this is a good time to do a bit of marking. I did spend a lot of this time when the children were working independently drinking tea and talking to my TA, but there were times when we would use the independent working time for other jobs.

Noise in the classroom is a bit tricky, I think; some teachers have the classroom much noisier than I would, but all the children were engaged and getting on with their work, so noise levels are not always an indicator of children working or not. What you do need to be listening out for is the type of noise. If the noise in the class seems to be calm and controlled, then there is a good chance that it is a reflection of the mood and working atmosphere in the classroom. If the sound of the noise is chaotic and rowdy, then you can bet that the children in that class are not doing their work; they are what we technically call "fucking about". And a very effective way of stopping a class from "fucking about" is to get them silent using the method I have explained, and then to insist that they continue to work but in silence. Obviously, once you state the expectation of total silence, then you have to follow through and jump on the first kid that talks. And you just know it is going to be that child that never does anything wrong, so you are very reluctant to sanction that particular child but you know what, you are going to have to. Otherwise the children will think, and rightly so, that you say one thing but mean another. So, don't be soft, do what needs to be done.

Name on the Board

Somewhere in your classroom you need a space where you will write up the name of a pupil who has been warned about a particular behaviour but insists on carrying on with that behaviour. The traditional way to show this is by having a "sad face" displayed on your white board. Writing the child's name under the sad face is a warning. It shows that you have already given the child a verbal warning about their behaviour and it denotes that if they carry on, you will take the sanction to the next level.

The name-on-the-board system works as follows. A child is talking while they should be listening. You say their name and say: "Stop talking, you need to listen, that is a warning". If the child continues to talk, you say: "This is your second warning, stop talking. If you carry on talking, I will put your name on the board". The child continues, you do not say anything at this point, just write the offending child's name on the board under that sad face or whatever sign you have to denote a sanction. You should have already told the children how the "name on the board" system works. If the child protests, say nothing; it is not a debate. You have warned the child twice and you have clearly stated that the next time they talk, you will write their name on the board, and you have done that. You can say at this point: "If you carry on talking, I will put a cross next to your name". If a pupil gets a cross next to their name, they miss five minutes of playtime or break time.

This can be problematic at times if the session you are in is at the end of the day. For primary children, teachers cannot give them detention after school, so they will have to miss their five minutes the next day, which is not ideal because really you would like to start each new day with a clean slate.

If the child continues to talk, you will give them another cross, which is ten minutes' missed playtime. If they get a third cross, then you remove them from your classroom and send home a letter to their parents explaining why they were removed from your lesson. The child was stopping you from teaching. This letter is called "a lost chance letter". The pupil has three lost chance letters. The first lost chance letter is simply a letter home informing the parent of the child's behaviour and asking them to talk to their child about their behaviour. If the child gets another lost chance letter for a different offence, then the parent has to talk to the teacher about the child's behaviour. If the child gets a third lost chance letter, this could lead to exclusion from class for a day.

Pupils as Friends?

Many new teachers feel the need to be the pupils' friend. Why? Especially in primary schools, why do you want to have nine-year-old friends? And to be honest, the kids don't want you to be their friend, they want you to be their teacher. Their mates are not going to make them stay in at break time because they couldn't be arsed finishing their work. Their mate isn't going to tell their mum that they hit some kid at playtime. So don't be their mate, be their teacher. That doesn't mean you can't have a nice, supportive and caring relationship with your pupils, but you are the teacher and that relationship needs to be clear and distinct. Do not muddy the waters by trying to be their friend, you are not their friend.

This leads on to how to talk to children. There are two great mistakes that new teachers make: the first is to talk down to children; the second is to talk to them like they are adults. Don't patronise children but at the same time do not think they have the same emotional maturity as an adult, they don't.

If you find yourself in the situation where you need to tell a child that they have to stop doing a certain behaviour, do not make the mistake of asking the child why they did it. This just gives the child time to justify their actions – unless of course you want to spend all afternoon listening to incomprehensible nonsense? Often children do not know why they do what they do, they just do it; they often are responding to some perceived injustice and a child's idea of an injustice is that someone looked at them funny.

If you need to tell a child to stop doing a certain behaviour, then tell them that. Say, do not do whatever the behaviour is, again. Do not get into a debate or argument, just give the clear instruction. However, the behaviour you want them not to do has to be a concrete behaviour. For example, do not say "Stop messing about". What is messing about? Say, "Do not throw that pencil at Akmed again". Or, "Do not throw things in my classroom". Do not say "Stop being silly"; again, what does being silly look like? Say, "Stand still while in the line". Or say, "Do not wave your arms around in the air when you are lining up". I have heard teachers plead with children, "Please,

please stop doing such and such a thing". No, tell the child, "Stop doing such and such a thing". It is not a debate, you need to give clear and concise instructions.

Another mistake teachers make, and this is something managers do a lot, mainly because they have not much to do and they have to fill their time doing something. They "investigate" an incident during lesson time – big mistake. Children will happily talk forever about some stupid incident. "He said that, I said this, she did this, I said the other, they ran over there, I told him, she told me, I said this…" and so on and on and on. Of course children would much rather prattle on about rubbish than do their Maths or English work. I would, wouldn't you? If you are going to "investigate" an incident, do it out of learning time. It is amazing how the number of playtime "incidents" reduce rapidly when children realise that they will have to explain themselves during their break or playtime, not in lesson time.

When you talk to the whole class of kids, rule one, show no fear. Even if you are shitting yourself, you have to learn not to show that. Keep any teacher talk to a minimum. No one likes to listen to someone going on with themselves for hours; it's boring, no matter how interested you are in the subject. You have to learn to use your voice; after all, it is all you really have. Use your pitch, high and low, use your volume, soft and loud, and use your eyes, look at them. Look at different children as you speak, move your gaze from one child to the next. As you speak, name the odd child. "The Romans lived a long time ago, Rachel; they invaded Britain, Ali; they found a land densely populated with trees, Joe…" Doing this keeps the children on their toes because they rightly think that you may pick on them next. So they make sure they are listening to you, they don't want you to say their name as they are looking out of the window watching Mr Nohair shouting at the back of some poor five-year-old for not remembering to pick up his coat on the way in from playtime.

Sometimes as you talk to your class, you are looking at the whole class and not an individual. You need to do this too, but remember to also occasionally focus on an individual to keep the whole class attentive on you. Before you start to talk to the class, make sure that everyone is actually looking at you. This can take a few minutes, but it is worth doing because that way you can more easily keep the children's attention. So, you want to talk to the whole class. First, you use whatever method you use to get the children's attention. Then tell the children to put everything down, and I mean everything – pens, pencils, rulers, paper tissues, crayons, books, sweets etc. Then look around the class and make sure each child is looking at you. If they are not, tell that child to look at you. Say, "Look at me, I am going to talk to you". This process does take a few minutes, but it is worth doing; do not be afraid of taking a bit of time to get your children ready for whatever you are about to do. It is not "wasted" time, it is preparation time.

Think before you talk about what it is you want the children to know, do not just think "I will talk about the Romans". Think carefully about exactly what it is about the Romans that you want them to know about today, or what instruction you are giving the children. What is it you want them to do? If you want the children to line up, do not say "Line up". Say, "I want you to stand in a line by the door, no talking while in the line", because that is what you want. You may even have to say, "Line up, one behind the other". Never assume that children know what you are talking about because more often than not, they don't. If you want a group of pupils to go to the back of the classroom and weigh different amounts of lentils, say, "This group, go to the back of the class room and use the weighing equipment to weigh the lentils. Follow the instructions on the worksheet". Do not say, "Go to the back and do the weighing". The second instruction gives your pupils license to go to the back of your class room, grab stuff and have a competition with each other to see who can carry the heaviest weigh.

Sanctions

OK, so there will always be a few children who will mess about in your lessons. They will push you, they will see how you respond to their behaviour. Why they do this at this point doesn't really matter, the point is they do it. Now, unless they are part of that two and a half percent of children that for some reason just cannot fit into mainstream school, then there is no reason why this child cannot follow your instructions and behave in a way that you find acceptable. Having a "troubled background" is not an excuse for disruptive behaviour and to be quite honest, it is not your problem at this point. Obviously, if you do have children who have issues, and you will have many of them, then that does need to be addressed, but that is something that needs to be sorted out in conjunction with the SEND and the management team, not you alone.

So, this child in your class is disrupting your lesson. How to deal with it? You have an established reward system and a consequences system that all the children are aware of (more on this later). You look the child in the eye and tell them what you want them to stop doing. Do not say "Stop being naughty". What is naughty or messing about? Identify the exact behaviour; it may be talking to their partner while you are talking, it may be talking while they should be working, it may be throwing something across the room, it may be making a stupid face at another child, it may be waving their arms around in the air. Whatever the behaviour is that is disturbing your lesson, you identify it and tell the child to stop doing that behaviour. You tell them that doing the identified behaviour is stopping you from teaching and disturbing your lesson, and stopping other children from learning. Tell them that this is not fair on you and not fair on the other children. Children have a strong sense of fairness; they will often say, "That's not fair". Use their inbuilt sense of fairness to manage their own behaviour. Then tell them that if they do the identified behaviour again, you will carry out the sanction that you have already got in place for such an event.

For example, in my class the first sanction after a verbal warning was to put the child's name on the white board under a "sad" face. This was really a visual warning to the child (more on this later). Then you say, and this is the important part, "It is your choice. I do not mind what you do, but if you do the behaviour I have identified, I will carry out the sanction". The important part is that "It is your choice". You have given ownership of that child's behaviour to that child. It is not a personal thing, you are not concerned about their behaviour, so they are not annoying you or bothering you on a personal level, it is the rules of the class that apply to all the children, so it is fair and equitable. Give the child the choice to decide how to behave. They may choose to carry on disrupting your lesson. Therefore, do not engage in any way with the child from this point, just carry out the sanction. I will talk more about consequences of disruptive behaviour and escalating disruptive behaviour and how to deal with it. Your rewards and consequences system must have already been built into what happens next. But remember at each step along the way of your behaviour scheme, it is always the children's choice. Hand their behaviour back to them. If they choose to behave in a disruptive manner, then so be it. You carry out the consequences of that behaviour. Do not worry, in time all children will comply with your behaviour expectations, as long as you have consistent rewards and consequences that you adhere to every day, all day.

Your sanction scheme must be able to deal with escalating disruptive behaviour. If a child displays behaviour that is disrupting your lesson and/or stopping themselves and/or other children from learning, then you have to intervene to stop that behaviour from continuing. I have outlined how to deal with such a situation but what do you do if the child persists with their disruptive behaviour? Let me say at this point that disruptive behaviour is anything that a child does that disrupts your lesson. Do not think that what is termed as disruptive has to be a major incident like chair throwing or fighting or aggressive verbal abuse. A child whispering to another child can disrupt your lesson, a child waving a pencil can disrupt your lesson, talking is a major disruptive issue during lessons.

But back to what is to be done with the persistently disruptive? Your sanction scheme must have escalating sanction criteria. Let's look at how the sanctions work.

Sanction one is verbal warning to the child and you telling the child to stop the disruptive behaviour. Sanction two: the child continues with the unwanted behaviour, you write the child's name on your white board under a sad face; you do not engage with the child, you just write their name under the sad face. The child knows they have been warned twice now, your verbal warning and this "name on the board" is the second warning. The child continues with the unwanted behaviour, you put a cross next to their name; this means they miss five minutes of their break time. The child continues, you put another cross next to their name; this indicates the missing of ten minutes of their playtime.

They are stubborn and continue, you put the third and last cross. Three crosses means a letter home to their parents explaining their disruptive behaviour and asking their parents to talk to the pupil about the fact that they have disrupted a school lesson. It also means the child is removed from your class to work in another class. This needs to be set up beforehand. You should have already negotiated with a few of your colleagues to have exchange places. They can send a child to work at the back of your room if the said child disrupts their lesson; equally, you can send a child to their class if a child disrupts your lesson. You may need a few colleagues on board because you may get more than one child that needs to be removed from your class. Let me tell you now, children hate to be out of their own class. The removal is only for the remainder of that lesson and the child can return in the next lesson. And sanctions start anew in the next lesson, any outstanding time to be missed due to name on the board and a cross needs to be noted down and the child misses their playtime/break time at an appropriate playtime. It may mean children doing their "time out" or "missing five minutes of break time" the next day when you have break time; this is not ideal but this is the real world. Let's recap:

Verbal warning
Write name on the board (second warning)
Put a cross next to the name (miss five minutes' playtime)

Second cross next to name (miss ten minutes' playtime)
Third cross next to name (letter home and removed from classroom)

I have used this sanction scheme for over 20 years and it works, so use it. There are other sanctions connected to "the name on the board", which is more about rewarding those children who always do the right thing and never get their name on the board. More of that later.

Rewards

Rewards are the most important element to any strategy you employ in your behaviour management approach. The rewards have to be something the children want. Do not give them a reward that you think is worthy and worthwhile for them. Do not think children will respond to a reward that is something you think is "good" for them. The rewards must be something they want. Build into your timetable part of the week where the children have "Reward Time". Make sure your reward time is at the end of the week. Last thing on Friday afternoon is ideal, but this is not always available due to curriculum demands. I have had my "Reward Time" on a Thursday afternoon. I ran my week from Thursday to Thursday.

But Friday afternoon is the best time for a reward session. Why? Simply because you can hold it over the heads of your pupils all week. You will create a "chart" with the names of all the children in your class on that chart. The chart will be divided up into the days of the week. Each day will be divided up into the sessions for each day. I had three sessions for each day. These were: before playtime in the morning; after playtime in the morning, and the afternoon session. Each child had their name on the chart, each child was awarded a "smiley face" for each session. I would mark on the smiley face for each child for every session. As the week progressed, the child could see more and more smiley faces on the chart. The aim for each child was to fill each section of the chart for the whole week. The idea behind the chart is that if a child has got a smiley face for every session during the week, then they can have their Reward Time. However, if the child fails to get a smiley face during a session, they will miss five minutes of their Reward Time for each smiley face missing from the chart. And yes, it is true that some children do not get any Reward Time; these children will be sent to another class with work during the Reward Time session. Your Reward Time should be about 30 to 45 minutes. You can't have your Reward Time lasting too long because the Head will demand that you do curriculum work during this time.

It is true to say that the Reward Time is not part of the curriculum and some may say, therefore, it is "wasted time", if there is such a thing as "wasted time". I would argue that the improvement in behaviour as a result of the Reward Time allows the children to focus better and achieve high standards because their behaviour is more task-focused and they are more motivated and engaged all of the week. The Reward Time is improving the educational standards of the pupils. So for me, it was a trade-off well worth doing. Thirty minutes on a Friday afternoon for a week of excellent behaviour and a class that is on task and engaged all week. It's a price worth paying if you ask me.

Reward Time comes in all different titles: "Golden Time", "Choosing Time", "Down Time", "Play Time"; whatever you choose to call it, the principle behind it is the same.

Reward Chart

Name	Monday	Tuesday	Wednesday	Thursday	Friday
Akmed	⚬ ⚬ ⚬				
Kelly	⚬ ⚬				
Nahella	⚬ ⚬ ⚬				

In the example above, Monday has gone well for Akmed and Nahella but not so well for Kelly. In the afternoon, she must have had her name on the board for some reason. Therefore, Kelly is already one "smiley face" or "football" or "circle" down. She won't be able to make that up. That means she has lost five minutes of her reward time. But what she can do is make sure she doesn't lose any more time. In the chart above, all the children got a smiley face or circle for Monday's Maths session, then after playtime, they all got a circle for the Literacy session. However, in the afternoon Kelly had a slight slip up and lost a circle. The next day as we add circles, you start from where you left off. See the example below.

Reward Chart

Name	Monday	Tuesday	Wednesday	Thursday	Friday
Akmed	● ● ● ●				
Kelly	● ● ● ● ●				
Nahella	● ● ● ● ● ●				

The next day you see that Kelly is still one circle down. That is because she lost her circle the day before; remember, she can't make it up. Once the circle is lost, it is gone forever. That may seem harsh but it means that not getting your name on the board is important. If you allow pupils to make up for lost circles, then you are opening up to negotiations, and that defeats the object of this reward system. Pupils will try desperately hard not to get their name on the board. They want their circles or smiley faces or whatever image you use. Akmed, the poor sod, had a bad day on Tuesday, he lost a circle in the Literacy session and the afternoon session. He is two circles down which relates to ten minutes' lost time in his "Golden Time".

Reward Chart

Name	Monday	Tuesday	Wednesday	Thursday	Friday
Akmed	● ● ●	● ●	● ●	● ●	●
Kelly	● ● ●	● ●	● ●	● ●	● ●
Nahella	● ● ●	● ●	● ●	● ●	● ● ●

We shoot forward to the end of the week. Friday afternoon, we look at our chart, one last reward just before you start your Reward Time, the last thing on Friday. Just before the children go home. The last half hour of the week. Look at the chart above – you see that Kelly was great for the rest of the week, therefore she misses just five minutes of her Reward Time. Nahella is that child that is always "good". She has her full complement of Reward Time. But poor Akmed, he lost another circle during the week, he is going to miss fifteen minutes of his reward time. Obviously, there can be times when children lose so much time that they miss all of their Reward Time. When this happens, I send the offending child to another class with work to do. They very rarely do it again. This system works, it rewards those children who always get it right.

Why does a child lose a "smiley face" on the Reward Chart? A child will not be given a smiley face if they have had their name on the board under the sad face. Remember, I spoke about putting a child's name on the board as a warning earlier. The idea behind this Reward Chart is that it rewards those children who always get it right. It is a positive reinforcement of acceptable behaviour. For example, if a child is talking in your lesson, you have verbally warned them and you have resorted to writing their name on the board as a stronger warning. When you write up the smiley faces on your Reward Chart for that session, that child with their name written on the board will not be given a smiley face. This system encourages children not to get their name on the board. Therefore, the name on the board is not just a stronger warning, it has a real consequence. More on consequences below.

Team Points

You want to have a few different types of reward systems working in your classroom at the same time. The one above rewards individual pupils for not getting into trouble. But you want to reward children for positive behaviour too. This reward approach uses a more collective peer pressure process. You will need to put your pupils into groups or teams. These can be based on table groupings – that is the method I use. Each table has a name or number. You can let the children make up their own name for their team. I often just gave each table of pupils a number, e.g. Table 1, Table 2, Table 3, etc.

The great thing about team points is that you can give out as many as you please. I'll explain why in a bit.

Write a list of all your teams and display them somewhere prominent in your classroom. It also needs to be easily accessible because you will be marking down each point you give to a team. I usually had my list of team names displayed on my whiteboard at the front of the classroom. Then I would use a tally system to record any points the teams acquired.

Team Names	Points					
	Monday	Tuesday	Wednesday			
Table 1	34	21	62			
Table 2	57	32	59			
Table 3	56	33	61			

The above chart is a simple example of the type of thing I am talking about. You may have hundreds of points per team by the end of the day. It doesn't really matter. The idea of this reward system is that you have a winning team at the end of each day. Although in some cases you may want to have a winning team at the end of each session. This is fine. You may want to have rewards given out more often to embed positive behaviour. Make sure each team does win at some point. You do have to manipulate the points so that all the teams do win. You don't want the same team winning all the time. Doing that demotivates the other teams. I always added up the team points after the children had gone home. I did this so that I could manage which team would win. If a team hadn't won for a little while, I would just give them more points at home time. The children will add up the team points themselves, so I would say I am giving points for how we leave the classroom. This then gave me the opportunity to add more points to a team that hadn't won for some time.

I also always manipulated the team points so that the winning team won by one or two points. This way you can tell the children that if only they had "shown active listening", they could have got a point and their team would have won, for example. This way it motivates the children to get reward points because they believe that just one point could mean their team wins.

Stickers

Stickers are one of the main positive reinforcement tools. Younger children just love to be given a sticker; they will stick their sticker on their jumper and wear it with pride. They will go through the day attempting to get more and more stickers until their jumper is totally covered in stickers. It doesn't really matter what the sticker is or what image is on the sticker, children love stickers. They love to collect them, wear them, show them off and boast about them. Sadly, as children grow up, the fascination with stickers wanes; it doesn't go away completely, but stickers tend to have less of an impact then when the children were younger. I am thinking of children from Year 4 upwards. I am not saying that these children will not respond to stickers and stop seeing them as a positive reward, but the child's desire to get a sticker at any cost does decline. Therefore, you will need to add value to your stickers. Give the pupil a reason to want to get given a sticker by you. Give the stickers surplus value. One way you can do this is by giving the stickers a value in terms of your reward scheme. Let me explain.

You should be running a team points reward system. I've explained this above. To give your stickers and to give the pupils an incentive to behave in a way that will result in them being given a sticker by you for appropriate behaviour, all you have to do is say that each sticker the pupils get is a point for their team. The pupil will want the sticker because it means more points for their team.

Other pupils on their team will encourage them to behave in a manner that could result in them getting a sticker.

I often gave stickers while the children are walking in from playtime or assembly – these times are crucial. The walking in from playtime is an important wind-down time, a time when the pupils come in from playing and turn their energy into positive focused engagement in your lesson. If you allow a rowdy mob to walk from playtime into your lesson, you will have a rowdy disengaged class.

There are times when you will want the children in your class to behave even better than they usually do. Times like "singing assembly". Assembly can be problematic, children will use this time to have a chat or just be fidgety. I found that if I offered double points for a sticker and then tell the children I will give stickers for appropriate behaviour in the assembly, this had a positive impact on the pupils' behaviours.

Stickers are not the only thing that can be given to pupils for rewards. Some teachers use a "comfy cushion" as a reward. The pupil that has the most reward points at the end of the day can sit on the comfy cushion for the day. Or you can have a soft toy that is used for a reward – the pupil that gets the most reward points gets to hold the soft toy for the day. And for older children, some teachers use money or shopping vouchers as a reward.

Consequences

There should be a consequence if a child is displaying negative behaviour. The consequence doesn't have to be anything harsh. A consequence can be a look or the removal of an object that is causing annoyance. Also, the consequence needs to be in line with the behaviour and consistent with any previous consequence. So for example, you do not want to exclude a child for the day because they talked while they should have been reading. At the same time, you do not want to give a child a stern look if they have just punched someone in the face. There needs to be a level of severity of the consequence that depends on the action or inaction of the pupil. I have already talked about some of the types of consequence that you may dish out – "name on the board", "stern look", "move the child to a different table to work", "remove the child from the classroom". I would always have an "isolation" table in your classroom. A table that is on its own, away from the main bulk of the class. This need not be the "naughty table", it is a place where a child can work who needs to work alone without the distraction of other pupils. Some children find it very difficult to work with other children. It is sometimes useful to move a child to the isolation table before any disruptive behaviour starts. Say to the child, "I am not moving you because you are in trouble. I am moving you to help you. To help you do your work". The main thing with any consequence or sanction is that it is consistent.

Rights and Responsibilities

Schools nowadays have a thing about "Children's Rights". You may have these in your school. Or maybe you follow or are part of the UNICEF Children's Rights Charter. This can be a useful tool in your armoury for behaviour management. In the UNICEF Children's Rights Charter, there is a long list of rights. However, the ones you want to use are "the right to relax and play" and "the right to an education".

"The right to relax and play" is very useful when it comes to playtimes and games sessions. Basically, it works like this. A child kicks another child, you say to the offending child, "You are stopping the child you kicked from having their right to relax and play. Therefore, because you are stopping that child from accessing their rights, you (the offending child) must sit out for five minutes' (or for the whole session, whatever you decide is appropriate for the offence)". Also tell the offending child and the rest of the class that they have the responsibility to behave in a manner that allows other children their rights.

Therefore, anything you deem as an action or behaviour that will disrupt the access to the children's rights can be sanctioned in some way. You can also add in the element of "reflection sheets", which children hate to do. A "reflection sheet" is a written account by an offending child of what they have done wrong and how they can behave in the future so they do not repeat the negative behaviour. The theory of course behind the reflection sheets is that it gives a child the opportunity to reflect on their behaviour and modify it in a way that is not disruptive. Liberals love this shit. Children hate it. Reflection sheets are used as a punishment and not as a method to help the child assess their own behaviour and its negative consequences. You will often hear a head teacher or deputy head shouting at a child, "Go and write a reflection sheet." the child sloping off in disgust at his bad luck for being caught. I do not use reflection sheets, but I can see their usefulness.

The next children's right that is very useful is "the right to an education". Obviously this right can be used at any time in school. A child does something to disrupt your teaching. "You are stopping the rest of the class from having their right to an education". You give the child a verbal warning, telling which behaviour you find offensive – talking, chewing, shouting out, throwing a book, walking around the class or any of the million things children do in school. You can then go on to say to the child, "You have a responsibility to behave in a way that allows these children to learn or be educated".

Another good children's right that is very useful is "the right to be heard". This right is particularly good when children are talking while you are talking. You say to the talkative child, "I have the right to be heard too". You go on to say, "You talking while I am talking is stopping me from having my right to be heard". You can also say, "You have the responsibility to shut up while I am talking so other children can hear me, so that I can be heard".

Reward System

The most important element in your behaviour strategy is your rewards. I use a variety of rewards. I have talked before about "Golden Time" or "Choosing Time", a time in the week where the children can choose what they do. However, even this needs planning because many children will want to play on the computer or iPads or whatever is the new technology.

You may allow them to access the Internet, to play games, but you will need to monitor the children's activity on the Internet, despite "parenting controls" on access to the internet, children will know how to get around these. You don't want your children to go home telling their mum that they were watching porn at school and you don't want them to be watching inappropriate material.

Not all children will want to choose to go on a laptop or iPad in their reward time, some choose to do art or play outside if you can accommodate that. I have found the most popular thing children like to do is play games outside in the playground. But due to staffing and the demands on the playground area, that is not always possible. So, you will need to have all the resources available to allow the child to have a choice of activities in their reward time.

I also used biscuits as a reward, not much liked by head teachers and other pious staff members, who will witter on about healthy eating and the like, as they stuff their fat mouths with cream cake. I used a biscuit as a reward for the winning team of the day or winning team of the session. Biscuits are quick and easy to administer and most children love a biscuit; it can be eaten straight away in quite a speedy time – reward received and devoured. Obviously, you need to be aware of allergies and the like. You don't want one of your pupils to have a biscuit as a reward for good behaviour, their throat swells up, they fall to the floor choking and then they die. It does not work well as a good behaviour incentive.

Other rewards can be these "party gift" things you can buy. Kids love those small bouncy balls, toy cars, dolls, dinosaurs, toy animals, colour pencils, colour pens and markers and toy jewellery. The rewards I use are biscuits for the winning team, a team wins each day. Reward time is for all the pupils showing good behaviour throughout the week. Therefore, reward time is a once-a-week reward. I use the "party gift" type rewards once a week for attendance.

Another reward system is the raffle ticket system. Each time a child does anything "good" or that you deem reward-worthy, you give them a raffle ticket. All the raffle tickets are put in a box and once a day or once a week, depending on how generous you are feeling, you pull out a raffle ticket and that pupil gets a reward. You may have a system where you pull out two tickets at a time or five or however many you want. The pupils soon learn that the more raffle tickets they have in the box or jar, the greater their chance of winning and you slip in some Maths. The problem with this system is that it doesn't reward everyone who has shown good behaviour. A child could be a pain in the arse all week, do one thing that is worth a raffle ticket and win the reward. The children that work hard, behave well all the time, can end up with nothing. I do not use this system, but some teachers do.

The next and last reward system I will talk about is similar to the above raffle ticket method. It used to be called "marbles in a jar". The idea is that each time a pupil does something you want to reward – for example, sitting in their seat – you put a raffle ticket or marble in a glass jar. You keep doing this for each child over and over through the day or week. The idea being that as you give out marbles or tickets as rewards to various children, the jar or box of raffle tickets begins to fill up. Once the glass jar or box of raffle tickets has reached the top of the jar or box, the whole class wins a reward. Again, the reward must be something the children want, you may have decided the reward beforehand. It could be extra playtime, ten minutes playing out in the playground, it could be to watch a DVD, it could be a trip to the local park. The added advantage of the marbles in the jar scheme is that if you have a child who is finding it difficult to follow accepted behaviour – and you will have several of these children in your class – you can give those children double the marbles or raffle tickets. You will explain to the whole class that you are giving your naughty boy Kenneth (don't call him that obviously) double each time he follows your behaviour expectations because he finds it hard to behave in a way that allows other children to have their right to an education, but in giving him or her double, everyone will benefit because the whole class will win the reward once the jar is full of marbles or the box is full of raffle tickets. Therefore, Kenneth getting double raffle tickets or marbles means everyone in the class will win the reward more quickly. Kenneth's class mates will soon realise that making sure Kenneth "gets it right" benefits them all and they will "encourage" him to behave in a way that you want.

The bottom line for any reward is that the pupils desire that reward. But your most powerful reward is your attention, so use it carefully and selectively. Only give your attention for positive behaviour. I know sometimes this is impossible, but bear in mind when you are giving a child your attention for negative behaviour, to balance that by giving more of your attention to the children who do display positive behaviour. Remember, for every negative comment you make, do three positive comments straight away.

For the most stubborn of children who just find it really difficult to behave in a manner that you desire, there is what I call the "Double or Nothing" reward approach. This approach is based on some research into addictive behaviour – why do people keep gambling, for example, when experience has shown them time and time again that they will be worse off at the end of the day. It is based on the idea that receiving a positive reward at random intervals is more addictive for humans than if you get a reward every time you hit the criteria for the reward. Computer games are based on this principle, and we know how addictive they are. I suppose it is the application of the uncertainty principle. For example, you are walking your children in from playtime, they are walking in a line, which you want, you also want the pupils to not talk while they are walking into your classroom. I would stand at the door of my classroom and as the pupils pass me to walk into the classroom, I give a sticker to the pupils that are not talking, but I do not give it to every child that is not talking, some of them I missed out deliberately. This has the effect of making the pupil desire the reward even more and they try a little harder next time to get the reward. It may seem harsh, but you should remember the pupils you haven't rewarded this time and make sure you reward them next time.

The "Double or Nothing" reward is where you set a task, completing a Maths worksheet or a word problem, for example. You inform the children that when they have completed the task and if the task is correct, they will be given a reward. Let's say in this case 20 team points. However, you tell them that you have an extra work sheet that they can complete if they wish, and if they complete this sheet, they get double the reward points. However, if they fail to complete the second worksheet, they do not get any points, and they lose the points for completing the first sheet. The pupils must be given the choice to opt into the "Double or Nothing" rewards. They can just opt to have the rewards from completing the first sheet, the 20 points. But if a child does decide to go for the double or nothing, then they must complete the second sheet correctly or lose everything. Again, this is based on computer game psychology. Not all children will opt for the "Double or Nothing" rewards. For those children, you will give them some points for completing the second sheet but it will be less than the "Double or Nothing" challenge. It is strange, but I found that the pupils who respond most positively to the "Double or Nothing" challenge are those pupils with the most challenging behaviour.

Working with Your TA

The most important person in your classroom, other than the kids, is your teaching assistant. At the time of writing this, teaching assistants (TAs) are fairly common in most schools, both primary and high schools, although they are deployed differently in each school. It is not uncommon, at the moment, for each class teacher to have their own TA working alongside them in the classroom for most of the school day. This is the case for the primary sector; high schools are different. I will be discussing working with your TA in a primary setting. However, before I continue, it must be said that primary TAs playing the role they do at the moment may fast become a thing of the past. Already, there are schools which do not use TAs, or the TA role is a shared one between a few class teachers. But the basic ideas I will talk about are still relevant.

First of all, your TA is not your personal assistant. They are not there to make you cups of tea, mop the floor after you or tidy up your messy desk. The TA is a teaching support worker. You are not their boss. You and your TA are a teaching team. I always referred to my TA when talking to the children as a teacher. I would say that we had two teachers in the class. This helped the TA because it gave them teacher status in the eyes of the pupils, so at those times when the TA had to take the class by themselves, they should be able to command the same level of respect that the children give you. Assuming of course that you have followed my suggestions in this booklet.

Your TA is a precious and valuable asset in your classroom, probably the most important asset you have. So, make sure you treat her or him well. Look after your TA, cover their back, support them and always be very, very positive towards them. Tell your TA how good they are and how much you appreciate their efforts. At the end of each term, buy your TA flowers or a bottle of wine or other culturally appropriate gift to show your appreciation.

Failure to support and care for your TA will lead to a disaster. Your TA can make or break you. You need your TA for your behaviour management. They can see the things you miss, they can keep on top of the kids while you are off explaining how the water cycle works or why humans drew cave drawings. You cannot have your eyes everywhere, so an extra pair of eyes is essential in your battle for behaviour control.

It is very easy for a TA to undermine you in the classroom. For example, a pupil makes a comment in earshot of the TA; if the TA is pissed off with you because you made them mop the floor and spoke to them in a rude manner because you didn't get laid the night before, they will get you back and ignore the comment. The pupil takes the TA ignoring their behaviour as a sign that it is OK for them to make comments. The pupil makes more comments and more exaggerated comments; the other pupils who have heard the comment respond back in kind. Within a few moments, your well-planned and exciting lesson has deteriorated into chaos. Instead of you teaching your brilliant lesson, you are now spending the afternoon sorting out who said what to whom and why, and writing letters home and giving out sanctions. And if that happens in an observation, you are stuffed. Therefore, keep on the right side of your TA. Treat your TA with utmost respect.

The TA will have a different relationship with the pupils, nurture this, you want a different perspective on what is happening in your classroom. Some pupils will confide in your TA and not you. Do not take this as undermining your authority, use this different relationship to gain a greater understanding of what is happening between your pupils. Many TAs are from the local community, they may be mums or dads of children in the school. If they are from the local community, they will know many of the parents and the children. This can help you massively when dealing with parents and pupils. Your TA will probably have a better understanding of the parents and the pupils than you. Your TA will probably have a greater insight into the relationship the parent has with the school. All this information will help you and assist you in your dealings with your pupils and parents.

There will be times when you will need your TA to do work for you that isn't supporting directly in the classroom with your lessons. You may need Pupil Assessment papers photocopying. Give your TA the time to do this task, do not expect them to do these types of task after school or at dinnertimes. I always gave my TA time during the lessons to go and photocopy. I took the class and she did the photocopying.

If your TA helps with marking, give them time in the lesson to mark the books. I do not mean every lesson, but there will be sessions where you can take the whole class by yourself and that lets the TA do those tasks that take a lot of time or concentration.

There are different ways to deploy your TA. Some schools have a diktat from the management as to how TAs are used in the classroom. Other schools allow you to act professionally and allow you, in discussion with your TA, to work out the best strategy to engage the pupils and get the best results for how your TA works with the children.

I had two main approaches. One was to allocate a group of pupils that the TA would support. This may be based on academic achievement, or lack of it, or behaviour considerations. Do not dump all the "naughty" kids on your TA and send her or him out of the class to work with the naughty children in a tiny, cold, damp and cramped room. I would often take the more "difficult" children as my target group and ask the TA to work with the other children. The TA's main task would be to keep the children on task and support the children with any difficulties that they might come up with during the course of their work. The children that I targeted for the TA to support were the more able children that I knew would probably be able to get on with the work or task. In this case, I would expect the TA to float between the target groups I had allocated to them.

Other times I would ask the TA to just "float". In other words, I would expect the TA to move around the classroom keeping an eye on the children, making sure they were on task and dealing with any issues that arose while the children were working. I would be doing the same thing, so we would be working as a team, talking to each other about any issues that came up or how we thought the children were responding to the task and if they had succeeded in the task that had been set. Often we would both mark as we were monitoring the children at work. This is an excellent way to mark, I believe. You can directly talk to the child about their work, sort out any issues with them and set them a task to extend their understanding or to consolidate their knowledge or to give them support in achieving that task.

The main point is to work with your TA as an equal. Work as a team, you are not their boss, you are their work colleague. A good TA can make you look great; a pissed off TA can mash you up and throw you out of the window. You don't want that.

Rebecca – A Case Study

Rebecca is a pupil in your class. Rebecca is not a real life child, but she is sitting in your class right now. You will recognise her, her attributes, her abilities, her attitude and her behaviour. There are probably many Rebeccas in your class, I would say at least five, probably more. Rebecca is not exclusively female; I just like the name Rebecca and I am following the tradition of referring to school pupils as she, not he. Rebecca's age range is from Year 1 to about Year 10 or 11, but she exists in all year groups. However, as she slips into teenage-hood, she becomes more complex but she is still Rebecca. And I will show you how my positive behaviour programme gave Rebecca the opportunity to flourish into that wonderful young person she may not have become.

Rebecca isn't "naughty". But then again, as I have said before, no child is naughty, whatever naughty means. It is more that her behaviour is not conducive to the situation she is occupying at the moment. Singing is not naughty behaviour or more appropriately, singing is not disruptive behaviour, when Rebecca sings in assembly along with everyone else and she sings the same song that the rest of the assembled school is singing. Or when Rebecca sings in the playground or school yard and she sings for the pure pleasure of singing and she sings a joyous song of youthful anti-establishment, this is her duty, her right, her expression.

But when Rebecca sings *I'm a Believer*, the song her class have been practising for "singing square" – and don't get me started on the uselessness of singing squares – in the middle of a science lesson about friction, then her singing can become disruptive behaviour. Rebecca isn't disruptive, her behaviour is.

Golden Rule: Do not categorise a pupil based on their behaviour. The pupil, like all humans, is much more than the snapshot of behaviour they display when in your care. You are not a Prevent operative, you are an educational professional. So don't fall into the simplistic and flawed Prevent mind-set. Your pupils are deep oceans of creativity, emotions, experience and talent – expressed, expressing and potential.

But Rebecca isn't that child, student or pupil that sings *I'm a Believer* in the lesson on friction. Rebecca doesn't throw chairs, or tell you to "fuck off", or stab her "friend" sat next to her in the hand with a newly sharpened pencil. Nor does she cut the hair of Amelia, who has, or had, long beautiful shiny black hair, using those "safety" scissors which enable the user not to cut paper or anything other than butter. Rebecca's "safety" scissor skills didn't mean that Amelia's mum threatened to sue the school because of Amelia's new hairstyle which, if only Amelia's mum looked at it objectively, she would see that if she now sent Amelia to school in a pair of Dr Martens and a hoody, Amelia's "bedhead shaggy spiky bob" looks great.

No, Rebecca isn't that student. Rebecca doesn't fight or use Anglo-Saxon expletives. She doesn't verbally abuse other pupils or throw pens, pencils or books across the classroom. She doesn't draw on other students' work, or steal or constantly need to use the bathroom, or randomly get out of her seat and wander around the class disturbing other pupils and she doesn't refuse to do her work. She does sometimes stroll nonchalantly to her class line, at the end of playtimes, just a little late, not so late that she'd be accused of deliberately ignoring the end of break time signal but late enough so that you'd notice. Rebecca is what we call in the business a 'nice girl or boy'.

So, who is Rebecca? Rebecca is that child who doesn't quite make the national expectations required of her for her age. She almost, but never quite, gets to the required attainment stipulation. And let's not get started on "national expectations" or "levels" or "mastery" or "proficiency" or whatever new and trendy term the Government decides they will be using this year. Because, as we know, these so called "attainment" requirements for our students are based on what? A quick scan of the students' academic results of some far-off country and usually a country that just happens to comply with the said education minister's political outlook, a minister who then decides to impose that academic model on our poor unsuspecting pupils and parents, who have to sit back and endure years of stress, heartache and failure. Then to top it all, we, the teachers, are blamed for the Government's stupidity. But like I say, don't get me started.

Rebecca, you feel, could easily reach those educational expectations. She comes across as a bright, intelligent and interested girl. She is engaged, her mum attends parents' evenings. Rebecca is clean and well presented. Rebecca's mum is a single parent, which is the norm in this neighbourhood. Mum is supportive of the school and always responds positively to any requests of her. However, Rebecca is like a leaf that very gently falls off an autumn branch, on to a still and tranquil pond. The leaf lands without a sound, unnoticed and unannounced, it is a beautiful graceful landing on to the water's surface. Inaudible and dark matter like, the leaf's landing on the calm and serene pond has startling and, for you, disturbing ramifications. As dark matter, which has never been directly observed; however, its existence would explain a number of otherwise puzzling behavioural consequences. Rebecca talks incessantly.

Rebecca sits on a table with three other girls and two boys and as demanded by the school management team, the table groupings are attainment related. In other words, the classroom is streamed based on academic achievement. The kids' view it like this: the clever kids' table, the nearly clever kids, the average kids, two of those tables, and the not clever kids. The pupils come to view themselves in this way too. The child sat next to Rebecca often cries and doesn't finish her work and complains that she is being disturbed and can't concentrate on her work. The boy sat across from Rebecca gets into trouble for making unkind comments to and about Rebecca. Another pupil will frequently stop and put her hands over her ears and refuse to work. The pupils on the table next to Rebecca will laugh out loud at something that has been said on Rebecca's table. A child on yet another table throws a pencil at one of the pupils on Rebecca's table claiming that a pupil from Rebecca's table has poked her with a pencil.

Another pupil sees the flying pencil and decides that it is flying pencil festival day and throws not just one but all the pencils on his table all around the room. A girl from the "clever kids" table stands up and shouts at the two pencil-throwing pupils to stop throwing pencils. A friend of one of the pencil-throwing pupils makes an abusive comment to the pupil who has stood up and told the pencil throwers to stop throwing pencils. The pupil who stood up to tell the pencil throwers to stop throwing pencils storms out of the class, slamming the door behind her, and stomps off to inform the Head Teacher. The Head Teacher arrives at your classroom to find two boys rolling around the floor, locked in what is known as a "bear hug", one of them desperate to bite the arm of the other. Pencils now rocket around in unvanquishable number. Rebecca's friend is sobbing, three of your pupils have decided to take an early morning break, five girls are now packed in the girls' toilet and with pupils from your neighbouring class joining them. One child has decided to walk around the classroom ripping up your work sheets, which will save you marking them I suppose. And one pupil has coloured their hand green using a felt tip pen. He likes the Hulk. You look on in total bewilderment, from calm to chaos in one small step for mankind.

Rebecca doesn't stop talking.

My behavioural management plan will avoid the above scenario. Creating an environment that minimises unwelcome behaviour is a far better policy than one which responds to behavioural issues as they arise. Also, you will have to deal with unexpected and uninvited behavioural hurdles. My behavioural plan not only helps you to create the physical environment to minimise unproductive behaviour but also helps you to create a positive social, emotional and intellectual environment.

I can guarantee you that if you follow my behavioural management scheme, exactly as I have set it out in this book, the above scenario will never happen in your classroom. Using the techniques that I have shown you, you will also be able to remedy the chaotic and anarchic sequence of events I describe above. The above situation may occur in your class if for some reason you have not been able to teach your normal class and a supply teacher or some other person has replaced you for the lesson. You return to your class to find a quagmire of unruly behaviour. "What is to be done?" as Lenin once said. The normal response is for the poor besieged teacher or teaching assistant to call for the cavalry in the form of the head or deputy Head Teacher or head of year. The cavalry will storm in all guns ablaze, shouting in that super low vocal pitch bass-baritone (two Es below middle C), which frightens the "bejesus" out of any living thing. This undoubtedly will silence the classroom. But as we know, it is a scientific fact that the more order we try to create, the more disorder we will actually create (in an enclosed environment, like our universe). The Head has restored order but in actual fact created more disorder because now the students know that they only have to respond to the Head Teacher, you have been carved out of the picture. The Head Teacher's action has had the effect of undermining any respect or authority you had with your class. And here I will again turn to Lenin and "patiently explain".

The classroom as described above is somewhat chaotic, however, if you have been using my behaviour management programme, remedying the situation is quite a simple matter. The trick is not to be drawn into the pandemonium, stay aloof from the hullabaloo that surrounds you. Quash your natural reaction to bellow at the students. The thing to do is to quietly whisper into Rebecca's ear, "The first table team that tidies up their table and shows me 'active listening' [see above for what is 'active listening'] will get double points".

Rebecca quickly informs her teammates that they need to tidy up and show "Sir/Miss" active listening to get double points. The energy that was being used to create chaos is now directed into creating order. Rebecca's team hurriedly sets to work, putting pencils back into pots and books in neat piles on the table, they sit, straightening their clothes, looking around to see if they are the first team to comply with my instruction. The other teams, seeing Rebecca's team tidying up, know something is afoot. They too imitate Rebecca's team, whispering to each other that they'll get double or triple points. One boy predicts that the class will be given extra play or break time. A new positive constructive atmosphere begins to materialise, the previous rancorousness being forced back into its dark damp cage, the cage door being tightly slammed shut.

Within minutes your classroom has returned to that happy state of equilibrium that we all strive to achieve in our work/life balance, but fail miserably.

Having said that, the point is you don't really want your students' behaviour to get to the point of chaotic breakdown. Avoidance is the best policy, I believe. To avoid the above scenario occurring, we need to look at pupils' behaviours in detail and determine which behaviours we need to deal with first. Break down the behaviour into parts and tackle one part at a time. Obviously, we will need to be doing this for several of the pupils at the same time. But with observation, analysis and self-awareness, the task becomes what you do naturally as a teacher.

Before we look at avoidance strategies, let's take a few sentences to analyse what happened with the introduction of my technique of whispering to Rebecca that "the team that tidies away first and can show me active listening will get double points". Obviously, for my technique to work, it would need my behaviour programme to be up and running in your classroom. Taking that as a given for now, just think what happened to the behaviour of the children in the situation that was described above; from an unruly mob, they became a well-ordered, attentive and engaged group of pupils. And the most important thing was, they did it through their own behaviour. I didn't direct them; they took it upon themselves to radically change their behaviour pattern. They took control of their own behaviour. Yes, the motivation for the change was triggered by my intervention and the possibility of some kind of reward, but having said that, the process that took place was one of the pupils themselves changing their behaviour from disruptive behaviour to positive, engaged and orderly behaviour. They not only decided to moderate their own behaviour, they encouraged other pupils to also become orderly and attentive. That is the power of my behaviour programme, it gives back to the pupils the opportunity to take control of their own behaviour and to shape their own learning. The impact of this behaviour programme is that it empowers pupils, it allows them to make choices. Let me dwell a little longer on this idea of students making a choice about their own behaviour.

It is important that as an educational professional, when you are dealing with or talking to students, you do not allow their disruptive or negative behaviour to have an emotional impact on you. Remember, a pupil's behaviour is not a personal attack on you. Actually, their behaviour is not personal at all, the classroom isn't all about you. You need to be supportive, caring and encouraging, but don't fall into the trap of allowing an individual pupil's behaviour to impact on your emotional state. When dealing with a pupil or group of pupils that are or have been displaying inappropriate behaviour, this is what you should say to them. Give your students a choice, put the emphasis on moderating their own behaviour back onto the pupil themselves. So, let's think about "my friend" Rebecca. She has been talking again at times where it is not appropriate for her to talk and her talking has caused minor disruption but is still something that needs to be sorted out. This is what I say to her.

"Rebecca, you have been talking at times when it is not appropriate for you to talk, we have already discussed this and you know that it isn't appropriate for you to talk at these times". Rebecca doesn't deny that she has been talking. Here I have clearly pinpointed the behaviour that I want changed. I have not said to Rebecca you need to be a "good girl" or you need to stop being "naughty" or even worse, "Rebecca, you are a naughty girl". No, what you should do is separate the behaviour from the child. As a teacher, you have to be very clear and concrete about what behaviours you want changed, never be ambiguous. I then continue to say to Rebecca, "It is your choice, either you carry on talking and you [insert here whatever the sanction is] or you stop talking at inappropriate times and receive [insert your rewards here]". Say, "I don't mind, it is up to you, stop talking and get the reward or carry on talking and get the sanction". There, it is now Rebecca's choice, you have removed any emotional attachment from yourself. You have said you "don't mind" how she behaves, her behaviour is her choice. And she is aware or becomes aware over time that any behaviour has consequences. The consequence may be positive or negative. Rebecca makes that decision. The eloquence of a positive behaviour programme like the one I advocate in this book gives the young person the ability to take control of how they behave. And so the consequence of their behaviour is their choice, you are empowering your students.

A technique often used by teachers is to move pupils from one group to another if the teacher feels that the pupils as a group or a pair of pupils do not get along well. They move the pupils in the belief that splitting the pupils up or sitting them next to another pupil or placing them amongst another set of pupils will improve the pupils' behaviour. However, often this manoeuvre fails; all that happens is that you export the disruptive behaviour to another group of students.

I am not saying that you do not take some care on how you arrange your classroom, which also includes where students are working. I have often set out my class in such a way that I have positioned two pupils, whom I have been informed "just can't get along", so that they have their backs to each other and are as far apart from each other as is achievable given the layout of my classroom. Although I don't believe this solves the problem of why these pupils are unable to work together, at least it avoids disruptive incidents. Although, often what happens is that whatever the issue these pupils have between each other erupts at some other time and place. So, maybe it is best to try and tackle the issue rather than sweep it under the carpet, but sometimes avoidance can be a short-term solution while you tackle other issues. You can always come back to try and solve behavioural problems at a later date. Don't think you are going to be able to solve all the issues that arise in one fell swoop.

Coming back to Rebecca. At first, I had no indication that Rebecca was my "dark matter". At first, I thought that the pupil that sat at her table who was obviously "loud" and quick to react aggressively was the trigger. Poor kid, how having a loud voice can condemn you. I moved the pupil to a different group. However, the group that sat with Rebecca, who had previously been my "good" group, became disruptive. It was "low-level disruption" – talking, petty bickering and the like. At this point, I still didn't identify Rebecca as the "cause", I thought I had just got the mix of pupils wrong. So, yet another move of pupils to different groups. Now, one problem with moving pupils to avoid disruption is that the move itself causes a period of disruption as the pupils get used to each other. If you are going to move pupils as a strategy to avoid unwanted behaviour, then you need allow a few weeks to see if the groupings work. Or all you have done by moving the pupils around is create different conflicts to resolve. At this point, I realised that my rearranging and regrouping of my students wasn't helping, it was actually making matters worse. I stopped the regrouping strategy and decided to focus on my behaviour programme.

It had become obvious to me that Rebecca was a low level disrupter; her inability to stop talking at appropriate times was causing issues, not only for me but also for the other pupils she was grouped with. My task was clear: stop Rebecca talking when it wasn't appropriate. Rebecca was going to have to learn to talk at appropriate times. Her mum said, "Oh! She's a chatter box". "Chatter box" isn't an electro-biochemical condition that can't be modified.

I spoke to Rebecca and Mum, and explained that I was going to focus on moderating Rebecca's "chatter boxing". I did this so that both Rebecca and her parent were clear what I was doing. I told them that I believed that Rebecca would benefit from learning when and when not to talk. That her academic achievement would improve and that her friendship group would grow. I didn't want Rebecca to stop talking,

talking is an important part of learning. Equally, there are times when not talking aids learning.

I told Rebecca that I would set her a task each day and that if she achieved the task, she would earn double points for her team. I did this for two reasons, one to motivate Rebecca but also I knew she would tell the other pupils that she would get double points for completing the task. This meant that the pupils in her group would support her in completing the task because Rebecca was earning "group" points, which meant they all benefitted from Rebecca achieving the task. At the same time, if Rebecca did talk at an inappropriate time, I would firstly give her a verbal warning. I would say, "Rebecca, do not talk at this time, this is a verbal warning, if you talk again, I will have to put your name on the board" (see above for 'name on board' sanction). Rebecca knows that a name on the board is a five minutes' loss of reward time. Once I had warned Rebecca, I would immediately positively praise three other pupils for not talking, "Well done, Ahmed, for not talking". I would wait a very short time, only a few minutes and then praise Rebecca for not talking and award extra team points. Usually if you tell a pupil to stop doing something, they will stop for a short time at least. Use this time to praise the student concerned. "Well done, Rebecca, for not talking, you can have ten extra team points for not talking". Two rules here for you to remember; one, for every negative comment you make, make three positive comments and two, look to praise the pupil you have just been negative with. I know at times it is very hard to be positive towards a student who has been driving you crazy all week, but then you are a professional, act professionally and don't allow your personal emotional state to govern your behaviour.

The task I set would be a very easy one, which I knew she would achieve. The first task was for Rebecca not to talk for five minutes during a non-talking element of the session. Once she had achieved this task, I would extend the challenge, at each step following the method I used above. It wasn't long before Rebecca was able to stop talking at inappropriate times. In this case, within days.

I would also be using the same approach with other pupils. I would identify just one behaviour for each pupil that I wanted to change, and follow the model above. Within a few weeks, most of the low-level disruptive behaviour was eliminated. That's not to say that everything in my classroom was perfect; I still had those two or three children who needed special support and for those students I would use a modified version of my behaviour programme. For some pupils I would use an adaptive variant of the behaviour programme and maybe one that was a stand-alone programme just for that individual pupil. But these pupils are not the main target of my behaviour programme; my programme is aimed at 98% of your students, not the 2% who display extreme challenging behaviour.

In Rebecca's case, it's not true to say that she became the perfect student, never talking when she should have been silent; it is more that managing her disruptive behaviour became easy. By the end of the first term with Rebecca, all I had to do if she was talking when she should not have been talking was look at her or gently tap her desk. She knew and so did her peers. One last thing on Rebecca's talking. Notice I do not say "Be quiet, Rebecca". I say "Stop talking, Rebecca". It is possible to talk quietly and sometimes you want pupils to talk quietly. Be precise. If you want a student to stop running, do not say "Slow down", say "Stop running". And do not ask "Would you please walk?" Pupil replies, "Mmm, no! I think I'll keep running, thanks, bye." And off she dashes.

Another important aspect of behaviour management is consistency. Never make empty promises or empty threats. If you say you are going to do it, then do it. Most children live in a world of empty threats. It goes something like this. Natalya is playing a computer game – 'Oh, shite!' she exclaims. Her mother tells her to stop swearing. 'OK, Mum" says Natalya.

Natalya's mum has told Natalya a thousand times to stop swearing. But Natalya continues to swear while playing on her computer game. "Bollocks" says Natalya as her computer game character is annihilated by a giant green alien. "If you swear again, I'll ban you from that computer," says Mum. "OK, Mum," says Natalya. "Shit, shit, shit," says Natalya. "I have told you, if you swear, I will ban you from that computer," Mum shouts. Mum never bans Natalya and Natalya knows this. Natalya continues to swear.

Your students will be used to threats and promises that never materialise. If you do not hold true to your rewards and sanctions, you will reinforce the very behaviours you are trying to disperse. One of the worst-behaved classes I ever came across was created by the teacher. The said teacher had come to me asking for support which I gave him. He introduced my behaviour programme but never stuck to the rewards or the sanctions. When a team of pupils had fulfilled the requirement for a reward, he would not give them the reward. If a pupil reached a sanction, he would not sanction the pupil. I told him to scrap the programme because his inconsistency was making the students' behaviour worse. He'd be better off doing nothing.

Last thing on rewards: once you have given a pupil a reward, you must reward them, do not withdraw the reward at a later date, even if after you have given the reward, the pupil then engages in behaviour that is disruptive. Think of it this way, once you have earned your day's pay, it doesn't matter if the next day you are off work, you still get the day's pay that you have earned. Your employer doesn't say to you, "You worked on Tuesday but were absent on Wednesday so we are not paying you for Tuesday."

Interference

The road to hell is paved with good intentions. Rebecca's classmate Arthur had many varied and complex behaviour issues that needed my attention. I was slowly chipping away at them following my own behaviour programme. Over a period of four to five weeks, Arthur's behaviour had become less disruptive. However, the Head Teacher, Mrs McGhastly, took it upon herself to "help" with Arthurs' behaviour. Unbeknownst to me, she had promised him a remote control car if he was "good" for the half term. Arthur would often say to me, "Sir, am I being good?" or "Am I good?". He had no idea what "being good" was. Neither did I. I would always reply, "Arthur, you are always good, it is just sometimes your behaviour isn't appropriate."

As we neared the end of the first half term, Arthur received a low-level sanction from me for some minor incident. However, Arthur responded in a most explosive manner. He leaped out his seat and shouted that I was a "dick" and stormed out of the classroom, slamming the door behind him. I was quite shocked because the sanction I had given Arthur was fairly minor and he had received similar sanctions in the past and had accepted it as a consequence of his behaviour. He stormed back into the classroom, and the rest of the pupils stopped what they were doing to watch the scenario unfold. He ran out of the classroom through the back door and hung around, tapping on the window and generally disrupting the whole lesson.

I ignored his behaviour at this point. You'll need to learn to know when to "pick your fights". If I had confronted Arthur at this point, it would have just escalated the disruption. Instead, I focused on my class. I told them, "Ignore Arthur, carry with your tasks. I know it is difficult to ignore Arthur's disruptive behaviour, I will therefore reward you all with an extra five minutes' reward time if you carry on with your tasks and do not respond to Arthur." A spontaneous cheer went up at the idea of extra reward time. Arthur, hearing his classmates cheering, looked in through the window of the classroom to see the whole class calmly carrying on with their tasks. You could see that he was a little confused by his classmates' reaction. Why where they cheering, he wondered. He thought he was missing out on something. Arthur came back into the class, sat down and continued with the task he had been set. I didn't challenge Arthur at this point about his behaviour, I allowed him to continue with his school work. Well, think about it, what I really wanted was for Arthur to complete the task I had set him and he was doing this.

The session ended and then I told Arthur I needed to talk to him. I asked him why he had behaved the way he did. He told me that he wouldn't be getting the remote control car that Mrs McGhastly had promised him because he had been "bad". I told him that he would receive a sanction for his disruptive behaviour but that his overall behaviour had improved, so I would tell Mrs McGhastly that in my opinion Arthur should get the remote control car.

The problem with Mrs McGhastly's intervention was that it wasn't linked to definable, achievable tasks. And the reward wasn't progressive. He either got the reward or not, which meant that if he made one mistake in the course of half a term (six to eight weeks), he lost the reward, which is a ridiculous burden to place on a child. Essentially, Mrs McGhastly had set him up to fail. There are times when rewards need to be "success or fail". But this needs to be placed within the bounds of do-ability. If it isn't doable, then you will create a failure. For the remote control car reward to work, it should have been based on Arthur achieving a number of reward points or stickers or smiley faces or credits. By using a reward points or credit system, Arthur can achieve the reward right up to the last day and if he does have some slip-ups, he is still able to redeem himself. Obviously, I spoke to the head and asked her to refrain from "helping". My behaviour programme works, you don't need help from anyone. Just do what I have told you to do and you will have a beautifully behaved class.

Conclusion

In conclusion, don't become a teacher, it is a shit job, the money isn't that great, the hours are long, the workload is excessive, the management are aggressive bullies, your work colleagues will stab you in the back and your TA will report you for something they thought you said. The kids can be fun and the parents are OK mostly.

If you still want to be a teacher, prepare yourself for depression and stress. Your anxiety levels will explode, your social life will die and your relationship will crumble. You will not have time for your own kids and you will become obsessed with the minutiae of school life. You will become a consumed, boring twat. You will work, eat, shit, sleep. You will be forced to medicate yourself either through your doctor giving you anti-depressants or through drinking copious amounts of wine each night or through recreational drugs. Become a teacher, say goodbye to life.

Now that you have read this, at least the kids will be well behaved for you and they won't send you bonkers, it'll be your work colleagues and the management.

And finally, if you still become a teacher, join a union and go on strike.